Economics and You

By

Author: Kristen Girard Golomb

Editors: Mary Dieterich and Sarah M. Anderson

Proofreader: Margaret Brown

COPYRIGHT © 2012 Mark Twain Media, Inc.

ISBN 978-1-58037-624-2

Printing No. CD-404168

Mark Twain Media, Inc., Publishers
Distributed by Carson-Dellosa Publishing LLC

Table of Contents

Introduction

Economics and You explores real-world applications of economics in a way that is relevant to students today. The book breaks down topics such as the Laws of Supply and Demand into easy-to-understand examples that teachers, parents, and students can review together at home or school.

The easy-to-follow format of *Economics and You* facilitates planning for the diverse learning styles and skill levels of middle-school students. This book is divided into two parts. The first is a step-by-step introduction to the basic principles of economics.

The second is an in-depth, real-life simulation activity designed to reinforce the economic principles and basic mathematics concepts taught previously while introducing the students to the consumer world.

The economic activities come in many formats. Vocabulary and basic economic laws are introduced in bold in every lesson. Case studies, articles, graphic organizers, questions, puzzles, lists, and other types of activities are used to spark student interest. Many of the materials are suitable for whole-class use on the overhead projector. An emphasis is placed on using math skills in real-life situations.

In today's challenging economic times, ensuring that students understand the value of a dollar and what it can buy is vital to their long-term financial health. *Economics and You* helps to lay the groundwork for students to grow into financially responsible adults.

Name: _____ Date: _____

What is Economics?

"What is economics?" you might ask. **Economics** is the study of how we produce and distribute our wealth. In other words, economics is money and what we do with it. Goods and services are the products that satisfy our needs and wants. A **good** is any item that can be bought or sold. A **service** is any action that one person or group does for another in exchange for payment.

A **resource** is anything used to produce a good or service that can be used to satisfy desires. Resources are what we use to produce our goods and services. **Production** is the process of changing the raw materials of the resource into some economic good or service that can be used to satisfy desires.

Some resources are **plentiful**, and some resources are **scarce.** Oxygen is a relatively plentiful resource, and silver is a relatively scarce resource. Some resources are renewable, and some are nonrenewable. A **renewable resource** is one that can be replaced, either naturally or by man. A **nonrenewable resource** is one that cannot be replaced in a timely manner or at all by nature or by man.

Complete the following chart by filling in resources. Check whether each resource you listed is plentiful or scarce, renewable or nonrenewable.

Resource	Plentiful	Scarce	Renewable	Nonrenewable

Name: _____ Date: _____

Goods and Services

Use the phone book for this activity. The phone book is organized by category. Look at the categories that you find in the yellow pages. Are they for the sale of **goods** or **services**? List 15 categories under goods and 15 under services.

Goods	**Services**
1. _____	1. _____
2. _____	2. _____
3. _____	3. _____
4. _____	4. _____
5. _____	5. _____
6. _____	6. _____
7. _____	7. _____
8. _____	8. _____
9. _____	9. _____
10. _____	10. _____
11. _____	11. _____
12. _____	12. _____
13. _____	13. _____
14. _____	14. _____
15. _____	15. _____

Which of the goods and services that you listed above are **needs** (necessary for survival)?

_____

Which of the above items are simply **wants** (desires not necessary for survival)?

_____

Supply and Demand—Part 1

Supply is the degree of availability of an item, or, in simpler terms, the number of items ready for sale. For example, the supply of airplane tickets to Anchorage, Alaska, is the number of seats available on all of the planes that fly there each day. Two planes fly into Anchorage each day, and they can hold 56 passengers each. This means a total of 112 passengers can fly to Anchorage each day. Therefore, the supply is 112 seats.

= 112 seats (supply)

Demand is the usability of the item or how many people want to buy it.

To continue the example, the demand is the number of people who want to fly to Anchorage each day. If 100 people want airplane tickets to Anchorage each day, then the demand is 100.

x 100 = 100 passengers (demand)

If supply is greater than demand (more seats available than people wanting to buy them), it is called a **surplus.** Surplus usually causes the price of the item to go down. When demand is greater than supply (more people want to go to Anchorage than there are seats available), then you have a **scarcity.** Scarcity usually causes the price of the item to go up.

Name: _____ Date: _____

The Chicken Farm

There is one chicken farm in Cholesterolville. Farmer Yolkman owns 10 chickens. Each hen lays about five eggs per week. Farmer Yolkman sells eggs to 10 families. Each family needs one dozen eggs per week.

Use the words **high, low, surplus,** and **scarcity** to fill in the blanks. The words may be used more than once.

1. Approximately how many dozen eggs will the chicken farm be able to supply each week?

   _____

   Demand will be _____ for these eggs, so eggs will be in _____.

   This will cause the price of the eggs to be _____.

   Assume that Farmer Yolkman bought more chickens and expanded his chicken farm. He now has 30 laying hens. He still supplies eggs to 10 families who each demand one dozen eggs a week, and each chicken still lays five eggs a week.

2. Approximately how many dozen eggs will the chicken farm be able to supply per week

   now? _____

   Demand for these eggs will be _____, supply will be in _____, and

   cost will be _____.

Supply and Demand—Part 2

Sounds pretty simple so far, right? Well, there are just a couple of small catches. Read on. . . .

As the price of an item goes up, the supply of that item will also go up. This is called the **Law of Supply.**

Think about this. When tickets to Anchorage are scarce, the price will rise. We learned that earlier. But as the price goes up, more airlines become interested in scheduling flights to Anchorage. They see how much other airlines are charging to get there and become interested in flying there themselves to make more money. Therefore, more companies will schedule flights to Anchorage. There will be more sellers of flights to Anchorage, which will lessen the demand. Price goes up and supply goes up.

Similarly, let's look at the **Law of Demand.** This principle states that **as the price goes down, the demand will go up.**

Back to Anchorage. The new companies flying into Anchorage over-satisfy the demand for tickets, causing a surplus. This surplus causes companies to lower ticket prices in an attempt to lure customers to buy tickets with their airlines. As the price of the tickets goes down, what would you expect to happen? Right! More people will want to buy tickets because it becomes a better value—a "deal." But as the demand rises, fewer companies can afford to fly at this price, and the supply goes back down. Price went down, demand went up, and supply went back down.

Ugh! What a vicious circle! To review:

> • **Supply** = The degree of availability of an item (what's for sale)
> • **Demand** = The usefulness of that item (who wants to buy it)
> • **Law of Supply** = As the price increases, the supply increases. This means more sellers, yet fewer buyers.
> • **Law of Demand** = As the price decreases, the demand increases. This means more buyers, yet fewer sellers.

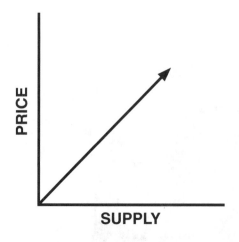

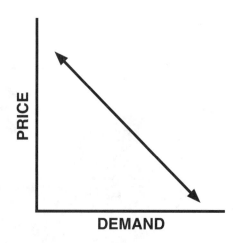

Pay Day

Employees are given a pay stub each time they are paid. A pay stub shows a person's earnings, the taxes withheld, and other deductions for a specific period of time. The employer is responsible for deducting or subtracting the taxes from an employee's earnings and sending it to the city, state, and/or federal governments. The employee receives a paycheck for the remaining amount of money. The following information appears on most pay stubs.

Gross Salary: the money earned by the employee before taxes and deductions

Federal Income Tax: the money deducted from the gross salary and sent to the federal government

State Income Tax: the money deducted from the gross salary and sent to the state government

OASDI (Old Age, Survivors, and Disability Insurance) or Social Security Tax: the money deducted from the gross salary and sent to the federal government to provide an income for the elderly and retired, families and survivors of the retired, and the disabled

Medicare Tax: the money deducted from the gross salary and sent to the federal government to provide health care for senior citizens over age 65 and the disabled

Net (Take Home) Pay: the employee's pay after all taxes and other deductions have been subtracted from the gross salary

Pay Stub Withholding Table

Yearly Gross Salary	Monthly Gross Salary	Federal Income Tax Withheld Monthly	State Income Tax Withheld Monthly	OASDI (Social Security) Tax Withheld Monthly	Medicare Tax Withheld Monthly	Monthly Net (Take Home) Pay
$10,000	$833.33	$61.25	$7.00	$51.67	$12.08	$701.33
$20,000	$1,666.67	$185.75	$43.00	$103.33	$24.17	$1,310.42
$30,000	$2,500.00	$310.75	$86.00	$155.00	$36.25	$1,912.00
$40,000	$3,333.33	$489.75	$129.00	$206.67	$48.33	$2,459.58
$50,000	$4,166.67	$698.08	$180.00	$258.33	$60.42	$2,969.84
$60,000	$5,000.00	$906.42	$230.00	$310.00	$72.50	$3,481.08
$70,000	$5,833.33	$1,114.75	$279.00	$361.67	$84.58	$3,993.33
$80,000	$6,666.67	$1,330.40	$330.00	$413.33	$96.67	$4,496.27
$90,000	$7,500.00	$1,563.73	$380.00	$465.00	$108.75	$4,982.52
$100,000	$8,333.33	$1,797.06	$429.00	$516.67	$120.83	$5,469.77
$110,000	$9,166.67	$2,030.40	$480.00	$568.33	$132.92	$5,955.02
$120,000	$10,000.00	$2,263.73	$530.00	$620.00	$145.00	$6,441.27
$130,000	$10,833.33	$2,497.06	$579.00	$671.67	$157.08	$6,928.52
$140,000	$11,666.67	$2,730.40	$630.00	$723.33	$169.17	$7,413.77
$150,000	$12,500.00	$2,963.73	$680.00	$755.00	$181.25	$7,900.02

Pay Day Simulation (Continued)

Career Cards

Directions: Duplicate this page. Cut apart and have students randomly draw a Career Card. The dollar amount shown is the yearly gross salary for the occupation.

Accountant $40,000	**Biologist** $70,000	**Restaurant Manager** $30,000	**Astronomer** $90,000
Meteorologist $40,000	**Lawyer** $90,000	**College Professor** $70,000	**Teacher** $40,000
Registered Nurse $50,000	**Airline Pilot** $140,000	**Computer Programmer** $50,000	**Bank Teller** $20,000
Policeman $50,000	**Flight Attendant** $40,000	**Waiter/ Waitress** $10,000	**Pharmacist** $80,000
Pediatrician $130,000	**Truck Driver** $30,000	**Farm Worker** $10,000	**Dental Assistant** $20,000
Architect $60,000	**Veterinarian** $70,000	**Mail Carrier** $40,000	**Cashier** $20,000
Barber/ Cosmetologist $20,000	**Physical Therapist** $60,000	**Secretary** $30,000	**Automotive Mechanic** $30,000

Name: _____ Date: _____

The New and Improved Chicken Farm

With one chicken farm in Cholesterolville and 10 chickens, Farmer Yolkman can produce approximately four dozen eggs per week. (Each chicken lays five eggs per week.) He sells one dozen eggs each to 10 families. Demand for these eggs will be high, causing the cost of the eggs to be high as well. Eggs will be scarce.

Answer the following questions in complete sentences.

1. Now that the cost has gone up, what will happen to the number of chicken farms in Cholesterolville? Why?

   _____

   _____

2. What will this do to the supply of eggs?

   _____

   _____

3. How will this affect the cost of and demand for eggs?

   _____

   _____

4. What will happen to the many chicken farms in Cholesterolville (the supply) as a result of the change in price?

   _____

   _____

5. Explain why this is a circular cycle.

   _____

   _____

   _____

   _____

   _____

   _____

Name: _____ Date: _____

Case Study: Auctions

Auctions are sales where the items are displayed and sold to the highest bidder. One day, you visit an auction in your town to observe the Laws of Supply and Demand in action.

The bidding begins with an old glass vase. The bidding starts low with an offer of $3.00. There are 15 bidders trying to place bids at this point.

1. Why are there so many bidders? _____

    _____

2. What is the name of this economic principle? _____

    _____

The 15 bidders have driven the price up to $27.00. There are now only four bidders remaining.

3. Why have so many bidders dropped out? _____

    _____

The second to the last bidder drops out at $51.00, and the remaining bidder gets to buy the vase for $51.00.

4. How did the large number of bidders affect the final price of the vase?

    _____

    _____

Everyone at the auction that week observes that the old vase sells for a high price.

5. According to the Law of Supply, what should happen next week? _____

    _____

    _____

6. After the Law of Supply takes effect, what will happen to the demand for and the price of old vases at the auction? Why?

    _____

    _____

    _____

Name: _____ Date: _____

Case Study: Write Your Own

Think about the economic concepts of supply and demand that you have studied thus far. Write a case study that will appropriately illustrate how supply and demand work. Explain **why** the Laws of Supply and Demand cause the changes you describe. Use an extra sheet of paper if necessary.

_____

_____

_____

_____

_____

_____

_____

_____

_____

_____

_____

_____

_____

_____

_____

_____

_____

_____

Name: _____ Date: _____

More Economic Terms

There are a few more concepts you should understand about supply and demand and how they influence the economy.

Consumption is the way we use the goods we produce to satisfy our wants and needs.

One group of people couldn't possibly produce all of the goods and services they use daily. Even if they could, the cost of doing so would be astronomical! Imagine if you had to grow the wheat, harvest it, mill it, transport it, and bake it all by yourself just to enjoy a slice of bread. So, instead, we rely on interdependence.

Interdependence is the way production and consumption of goods and services is divided among many different individuals and groups. Today we have farmers to grow the wheat, special machines to harvest it, mills to grind it into flour, and trucking companies to transport the flour to the bakers. Baking companies then bake it into bread, and truckers once again transport the bread to stores where it can be sold. Many other individuals are involved in producing the necessary machines, ingredients, and packaging. Duplication of effort and supplies is kept to a minimum. Each group specializes in one area of bread production. This division of labor saves time and money for all and keeps the price of bread down.

This system of interdependence requires some sort of exchange. We exchange **money** for the goods and services that we need. Mills pay farmers for the wheat, customers pay stores for the bread, and so on.

Put the following steps of production and consumption for paper in the right order from 1–8, with 1 being the first step and 8 being the last step.

_____ Lumberjacks cut down trees.

_____ Mill turns lumber into pulp.

_____ Truckers transport trees to the mill.

_____ Truckers transport pulp to the factory.

_____ Consumers buy paper from the store.

_____ Paper factory turns pulp into paper.

_____ Tree farmers plant seedling trees.

_____ Truckers transport paper to stores.

Name: _____ Date: _____

Case Study: The Lemonade Stand

1. Is this business selling a good or a service?

   _____

2. List the resources used to produce the lemonade.

   _____

   _____

3. Are these resources scarce or plentiful?

   _____

4. Are these resources renewable or nonrenewable?

   _____

5. List the steps in the production of lemonade.

   _____

   _____

   _____

   _____

   _____

Name: _____ Date: _____

Case Study: The Lemonade Stand (cont.)

6. This business is interdependent with what other businesses?

    _____

    _____

7. What is the actual pictured demand for lemonade?

    _____

    _____

8. What things could increase the demand for lemonade?

    _____

    _____

    _____

9. What things could decrease the demand for lemonade?

    _____

    _____

    _____

10. What would happen if the price of lemonade increases due to greater demand?

    _____

    _____

    _____

11. What would happen if the price of lemonade decreases due to a lesser demand?

    _____

    _____

    _____

12. What effect would competition (another lemonade stand) be likely to have on this business?

    _____

    _____

    _____

Money in the United States

Thousands of years ago, people **bartered**, or traded, for everything they needed. As civilization progressed, carrying around all the items one wanted to trade became burdensome and impractical. People realized they needed a standard unit of value to base their trades on. This unit needed to be small enough to carry easily, of widely accepted value, and difficult to copy. Coins, and later paper money, became this standard of value.

Coins were originally made of valuable metals. All coins of the same value were made of the same amount of precious metal. Today, pennies are made of copper-plated zinc. They are 97.5% zinc and 2.5% copper. Nickels are made of an alloy, a mixture of metals, that is 75% copper and 25% nickel. "Silver" coins (dimes, quarters, half-dollars, and dollars) are no longer made of silver at all. These coins are actually a copper core covered with the same copper/nickel alloy that is used in nickels. When coins are made, they are said to be **minted**. The U.S. Mint is the government agency in charge of making coins. Coins are minted in six different denominations (amounts) in the United States. These are the penny (1¢), nickel (5¢), dime (10¢), and quarter (25¢), along with the less-commonly used half-dollar (50¢) and dollar (100¢).

Paper money is officially called **Federal Reserve notes**. Originally, paper money was backed in silver or gold. That meant that you could take any one-dollar bill to a bank and have it traded in for its equal value in silver or gold. As the amount of money in **circulation** (money printed and currently being used) grew, paper money outgrew the country's supply of gold and silver. Now paper money is backed by the Federal Reserve and is protected in part by the Federal Reserve and in part by the government alone. Federal Reserve notes are printed in the following denominations: $1, $2, $5, $10, $20, $50, $100. Until 1969, the Federal Reserve also issued bills in the amounts of $500, $1000, and $10,000. With the prevalence of checking accounts and credit cards, these large denominations are no longer necessary.

Name: _____ Date: _____

Money Research Project

Use an encyclopedia, the Internet, real money, or other references to complete the following research project. Next to each denomination listed, state the famous figure printed on the bill and the illustration found on the reverse side.

In recent years, the U.S. Mint has issued coins with different famous figures and/or illustrations on pennies, nickels, quarters, and dollars. These programs honor states, presidents, historic events, and national parks. For an in-depth research project, concentrate on one type of coin and list all the current variations for that coin. You may want to create a poster or chart to display your information.

Bill Denomination	Famous Figure	Illustration
$1		
$2		
$5		
$10		
$20		
$50		
$100		

Banking and Interest

All the economic activity we've talked about so far revolves around one medium of exchange—money! Money buys goods, services, and resources. Money leads to consumption, and money is the motivation behind interdependence. Basically, money makes the world go around, just like the old saying goes!

Money is typically kept in banks for security and convenience reasons. People no longer hide their riches under floorboards or in mattresses. Instead, they deposit their money into a bank for safe-keeping and earn interest on it. **Interest** is the money the bank pays depositors for the privilege of "borrowing" their money until they need it back again. Interest is usually a percentage of the total money deposited in the bank. For example, a customer deposits $2,000 into a savings account at 5% interest. He leaves it in the bank for a year, and when he goes to withdraw it, he discovers that he now has $2,100! The extra $100 is interest.

Interest is one important reason that customers use banks. They can safely store their money, have access to it (through checks, ATM cards, and so on), and still use it to make more money without doing a thing! Sounds great, but what do the banks do with all of that money? You might imagine that they store it all in huge vaults piled floor to ceiling with stacks of five- and 10-dollar bills. If that were the case, how could they afford to pay everyone interest? Banks have to earn money somehow, and the way they do that is through loans.

A **loan** is money given to a borrower temporarily that must be paid back fully plus interest. People who need money (like for a house or a car) go to banks and ask for loans. These people promise to pay all of the money back in a certain amount of time, and they promise to pay the bank interest for this service (like a fee for lending them money).

Banks use the money deposited with them to make loans. Banks actually only keep enough money in reserve to meet their day-to-day requests for withdrawals. They loan out the rest. No bank could survive if all of its depositors decided to withdraw their money on the same day. They simply wouldn't have the cash available to pay them all. Most of a bank's money is usually tied up in loans, which are making money for the bank. Typically, banks charge customers higher interest on loans than they give customers on savings accounts. This helps them earn money and stay in business.

Name: _____ Date: _____

How To Calculate Interest

Interest = Amount x Interest Rate x Time

Amount is calculated in dollars, interest is calculated in decimals (5% = 0.05), and time is measured in years (1 year, 6 months = 1.5)

Examples:

You deposit $500 in the bank at 7% interest for 3 years. How much interest do you earn?

Interest = $500 x 0.07 x 3 = $105

You borrow $20,000 for a car at $9\frac{1}{2}$% interest. You pay it back in full 5 years later. How much interest must you pay?

Interest = $20,000 x 0.095 x 5 = $9,500

(**Important note:** Borrowers do not usually have their interest computed by the formula above. Most borrowers pay their debt back a little bit at a time. This reduces the amount of the loan still owed, which in turn reduces the principal, or the amount still owed. Interest for loans paid back a little at a time is figured using a more complicated formula. This is called **compound interest**. For the sake of simplicity, we will not investigate this kind of interest here.)

Use a calculator to compute interest on the following situations. Write the equation and the answer.

1. You deposit $1,000 in the bank when your son is born. If the money earns 5% interest, how much total money will he have saved for college when he is 18?

   _____

2. You loan your nephew $475 for $2\frac{1}{2}$ years. He agrees to pay 2% interest. How much interest does he pay you for the privilege of borrowing money?

   _____

3. You take out a short-term loan to pay for a trip until your income tax return arrives. If you borrow $250 at $8\frac{1}{4}$% interest, how much will you owe when you receive your tax return in 3 months?

   _____

4. What interest would you earn if you deposited $4,300 in the bank at 5% interest for 10 years?

   _____

The Federal Reserve

The **Federal Reserve** is the central bank in the United States. It is comprised of 12 Federal Reserve banks located across the United States and is headed by a seven-member Federal Reserve Board in Washington, D.C. The Federal Reserve was established in 1913 to strengthen the banking activities of the nation. The Federal Reserve not only insures all deposits made in member banks, but is the most important control over the money supply in the United States.

The Federal Reserve can affect the supply of money available in three important ways:

1. The Federal Reserve sets and changes the requirements on how much money banks must keep in reserve. This is the amount of cash a bank keeps on hand to fulfill their customers' day-to-day requests. Remember that the rest of the money in a bank is usually lent out to make interest. A bank's reserves include the cash on hand in its own safes and money it must put in an account at the Federal Reserve bank.

2. The Federal Reserve can buy and sell government bonds. A **bond** is a certificate issued by a government or business that needs to borrow money. They will pay the buyer of the bond back later with interest.

3. The Federal Reserve can loan money out to banks when they are short on reserves.

How do these things affect the money supply? Well . . .

1. Changing the amount of money held in reserve at banks changes the amount of money available to loan out. If the reserve amount is increased, then less money will be available for loans. This will decrease the demand for products, decrease production, and sometimes cause a cutback in workers and increase unemployment. This is called a **recession.** Decreasing the amount held in reserve will have the opposite effect. This will increase the amount of money available for loan and increase consumer demand for products (since they have more money with which to buy them). Increased demand will cause increased production and a greater demand for workers. This is called **inflation.**

2. The Federal Reserve can sell government bonds. Selling bonds will take money out of the economy as buyers pull their money out of banks to pay for them. This in turn causes a lesser amount of money to be available for loans. The Federal Reserve can also buy bonds to put money back into the banks and increase loans.

3. Loaning money to banks in trouble helps prevent everyone from withdrawing their money from a troubled bank all at the same time.

Name: _____ Date: _____

The Federal Reserve: Questions

Answer the following questions in complete sentences using information from the previous page.

1. Why was the Federal Reserve established?

   _____

   _____

2. How do Federal Reserve banks get their money?

   _____

   _____

3. What do banks do with the money not held in reserve? Why?

   _____

   _____

   _____

4. Why can't all depositors in a bank withdraw all of their money at once?

   _____

   _____

5. List three ways the Federal Reserve can affect the money supply.

   _____

   _____

   _____

6. Why do you think the Federal Reserve wants to affect the money supply?

   _____

   _____

7. What happens when too much money is in circulation?

   _____

   _____

   _____

8. What happens when too little money is in circulation?

   _____

   _____

   _____

Name: _____ Date: _____

Federal Reserve Banks

The Federal Reserve has 12 banks that make up the Federal Reserve system. These banks are located all across the United States. Decipher the scrambled cities below and correctly label them on the United States map.

1. SDLLAA _____ 2. AGCOIHC _____

3. NIATS UISLO _____ 4. OOTSBN _____

5. VEELLCDNA _____ 6. AAATTLN _____

7. EWN KYRO _____ 8. INASLOPNEMI _____

9. KSASNA YICT _____ 10. ASN OCCSAFRIN _____

11. HCNDOIMR _____ 12. HDAIPPELIHLA _____

Name: _____ Date: _____

Flow Chart: The Federal Reserve

The Federal Reserve increases the amount of money banks must keep in reserve.

The Federal Reserve

The Federal Reserve decreases the amount of money that banks must keep in reserve.

With less money to lend, banks _____ interest rates.

Member Banks

With more money to lend, banks _____ interest rates.

Borrowing _____ and spending _____.

Consumers

Borrowing _____ and spending _____.

Demand _____, production _____, and employment _____.

Producers/ Industry

Demand _____, production _____, and employment _____.

Inflation

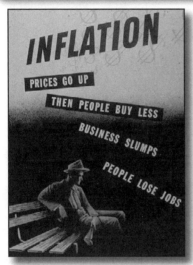

Inflation is a rise in the amount of money in the economy. Inflation usually brings about a rise in prices. This lowers the value of the dollar, meaning that a dollar buys less than it did before. Inflation can come about any time too much money is in circulation. The Federal Reserve often triggers inflation by buying bonds or lowering interest rates. Inflation is not rising prices as many people believe; inflation causes rising prices.

A recession is the opposite of inflation. A **recession** is when there is less money in the economy, causing a decline in demand. This will usually increase the value of a dollar, meaning that a dollar will buy more. A **depression** is simply a severe recession that results in a decline in business, high unemployment, and lowered stock market values.

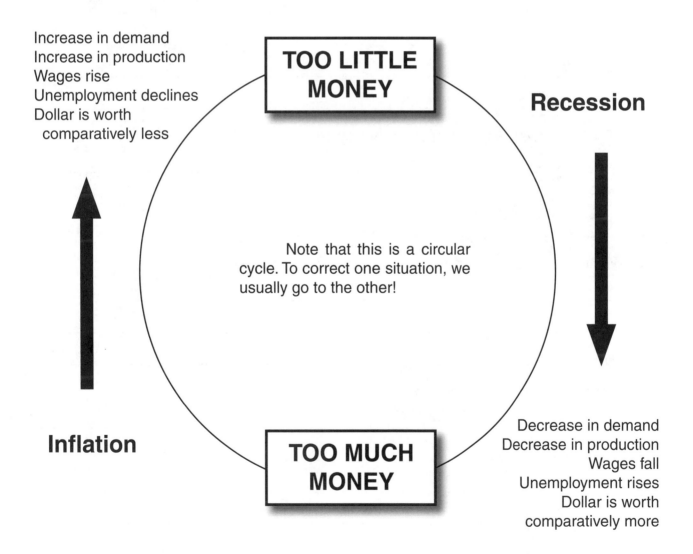

Increase in demand
Increase in production
Wages rise
Unemployment declines
Dollar is worth
   comparatively less

TOO LITTLE MONEY

Recession

Note that this is a circular cycle. To correct one situation, we usually go to the other!

Inflation

TOO MUCH MONEY

Decrease in demand
Decrease in production
Wages fall
Unemployment rises
Dollar is worth
comparatively more

Name: _____ Date: _____

Inflation: Questions

Answer the following questions in complete sentences.

1. What organization most affects the money supply?

   _____

   _____

2. Why is there a decrease in production during a recession?

   _____

   _____

   _____

3. Why is there an increase in production during inflation?

   _____

   _____

   _____

4. Why is the dollar worth comparatively less during inflation?

   _____

   _____

   _____

5. Why is the dollar worth comparatively more during a recession?

   _____

   _____

   _____

6. Explain why the cycle is circular.

   _____

   _____

   _____

   _____

Name: _____ Date: _____

Inflation Case Study: Real Estate

Balanced economy: No inflation

   In this economy, demand for houses is three (three people want houses). Supply is three houses, and the cost of the houses stays reasonable.

Recession

Supply = _____   Demand = _____

1. Does this economy have too little or too much money? _____

2. Does this cause the cost of houses to go up or down? _____

3. Why? _____

   _____

4. Does this mean that the value of the dollar has gone up or down? _____

Inflation

Supply = _____   Demand = _____

5. Does this economy have too little or too much money? _____

6. Does this cause the cost of houses to go up or down? _____

7. Why? _____

   _____

8. Does this mean that the value of the dollar has gone up or down? _____

Name: _____ Date: _____

What Did Things Cost?

How to compute percent of change in cost:

$$\frac{x}{100} = \frac{\text{Change in price}}{\text{Past price}}$$

Inflation, an increase in the money supply, causes higher prices. These higher prices diminish the buying power of the dollar. Use grocery ads or cash register receipts or visit a local grocery store to find out the exact cost of the items listed below. Then use the formula to compute the percent of change in price (due to inflation) from 1970 to the present. Show your calculations on the back of this page or on a sheet of scratch paper.

Item	Price in 1970	Present Price	Percent of Change
1 lb. apples	$0.25		
1 lb. whole chicken	$0.46		
1 dozen eggs	$0.67		
1 quart milk	$0.36		
1 lb. pork chops	$1.30		
1 lb. sugar	$0.13		
tea bags (48)	$0.61		
1 lb. flour	$0.12		
1 lb. margarine	$0.33		
1 lb. coffee	$0.91		

Prices taken from *The Value of a Dollar: Prices and Incomes in the United States, 1860–2009,* edited by Scott Derks (Amenia, NY: Grey House Pub.), 2009. Prices are New York City averages from 1970.

Name: _____ Date: _____

Case Study: Menus

The Dollar Deli
Menu

Grilled Cheese Sandwich	$3.00	$3.10
Ham and Cheese Sandwich	$3.75	$3.50
Turkey Club	$4.50	$4.00
Roast Beef Sandwich	$4.25	$4.50
Potato Chips	$1.00	$0.50
French Fries	$1.25	$0.75
Giant Cookie	$1.50	$1.20
Fresh Fruit	$0.75	$1.00
Soda	$1.25	$1.10
Milk	$1.00	$0.90
Lemonade	$1.05	$1.50

"Where your dollar always buys more . . . good food!"

The Dollar Deli decided to change its prices. Use the menu above to answer the following questions.

1.   Which menu items inflated in price?

_____

_____

2.   Which item inflated the most?

_____

3.   Which menu items deflated in price?

_____

4.   Which item(s) deflated the most?

_____

5.   You order a grilled cheese sandwich, potato chips, soda, and a giant cookie. What was the percentage of change in this lunch from the old menu to the new menu?

_____

6.   Was this change (question 5) an inflation or deflation in price?

_____

Name: _____ Date: _____

Economic Crossword Puzzle

Use the clues on page 27 to complete the crossword puzzle below.

Name: _____ Date: _____

Economic Crossword Puzzle—Clues

ACROSS

2. situation that occurs when there is too little money in the economy
5. amount printed on money
7. opposite of plentiful
8. money borrowed temporarily that must be paid back, usually plus interest
9. over-supply
10. the number of items available for sale
12. situation that occurs when there is too much money in the economy
16. the study of money
17. place to save and borrow money
18. not replaceable
20. any item that can be bought or sold
21. buyer
22. any action that one person or group does for another in exchange for payment
23. the main bank of the United States

DOWN

1. maker of goods or services
3. the way production and consumption of goods and services are divided among many different people and groups
4. a severe recession
6. the way we use goods and services
11. fee paid by the borrower of money and the fee paid to the saver of money
13. to make coins
14. the number of people who want to buy a good or service
15. replaceable
19. anything used to produce a good or service that will satisfy our wants and desires

---

Word Bank

bank	demand	resource
recession	interdependence	service
interest	supply	nonrenewable
consumer	consumption	economics
good	renewable	depression
loan	scarce	surplus
mint	denomination	producer
Federal Reserve	inflation	

To the teacher: For a more challenging puzzle, fold paper on the dotted line before copying.

Matching Quiz: Economic Terms

Place the letter of the definition in Column B on the blank next to the corresponding term in Column A.

COLUMN A	COLUMN B
_____ 1. bank	A. a severe recession
_____ 2. recession	B. to make coins
_____ 3. interest	C. any item that can be bought or sold
_____ 4. consumer	D. resource that is replaceable
_____ 5. good	E. institution for saving and lending
_____ 6. loan	F. fee paid when you borrow money and earned when you save it
_____ 7. mint	G. how people use goods and services to satisfy their wants and needs
_____ 8. Federal Reserve	H. buyer of a good or service
_____ 9. demand	I. the quantity of goods or services available for sale
_____ 10. interdependence	J. to lend out money temporarily
_____ 11. supply	K. over-supply
_____ 12. consumption	L. time when there is too little money in the economy
_____ 13. renewable	M. the amounts that money is printed in
_____ 14. scarce	N. hard to find; not enough to meet demand
_____ 15. denominations	O. time when there is too much money in the economy, resulting in higher prices
_____ 16. inflation	P. the study of the production and distribution of wealth
_____ 17. resource	Q. someone who makes goods or provides services
_____ 18. service	R. resource that cannot be replaced once it is used up
_____ 19. nonrenewable	S. how many people want to buy a good or service
_____ 20. economics	T. anything used to produce a good or service
_____ 21. depression	U. the main regulator of banks in the United States
_____ 22. surplus	V. the way production and consumption of goods and services is divided among many different people
_____ 23. producer	W. any action that one person or group performs for another in exchange for payment

Consumer Simulation

When practiced in isolation, math concepts often seem unrelated to the real world that surrounds students daily. This simulation is intended to spark student interest, integrate the economic ideas presented in the first part of this book, teach the basic principles of consumer education, and review all math operations.

To begin the simulation, each student is assigned an occupation and salary by random drawing. Each then figures his or her weekly gross and net salary (based on an estimated tax rate) and opens a checking account with his or her first month's pay. Students make their own checkbooks and learn to write checks and record expenses. The simulation continues through many other examples designed to help prepare students to enter college or the working world in an economically prepared way.

I believe that your students will find this simulation challenging, enlightening, and a whole lot of fun! It is fairly easy to manage and requires little out-of-class preparation once begun. For most class periods, a quick presentation of the problem of the day is all that is necessary before setting the students free. The teacher's role becomes one of loan approval officer, banker, and accountant. The math involved requires a working knowledge of percentages and decimals, and you might consider allowing students to use calculators during the simulation to manage lengthy computations. Additionally, teachers will need to provide two "bank" boxes—one for deposits and one for checks written. More will be said about this later.

Care needs to be taken in handling the natural differences in salaries that arise in the simulation. It is very interesting to watch students' reactions to their randomly drawn occupations and the inequality of their salaries (not to mention their perception of some careers as "male" or "female"). What may initially seem like a tremendous amount of money quickly dwindles, as adults all know! Carefully monitor individual checkbook balances to ensure that all students have an adequate amount of money to "live on" during the course of the simulation. It might be necessary to issue loans or even announce a sudden "lottery" winner!

Throughout the simulation, directions for teachers will appear when necessary at the bottom or side of the page. These can be folded under before copying the pages for student use.

Career Cards

All salary information for these career cards was taken from the 2010–11 *Occupational Outlook Handbook* of the U.S. Department of Labor—Bureau of Labor Statistics. Unless otherwise stated, all salaries quoted are the median or average figures of full-time salaried workers.

Accountant $59,430	Funeral Director $52,210	Restaurant Manager $46,320	Hotel Manager $45,800
Nuclear Engineer $101,500 (mid-level experience)	Civil Engineer $82,280 (mid-level experience)	Architect $76,750 (8–10 years experience)	Barber/ Cosmetologist $26,510
Meteorologist $81,290	Social Worker $43,850 (Child and Family)	College Professor $58,830	Elementary School Teacher $49,140
Veterinarian $79,050	Physical Therapist $72,790	Registered Nurse $62,450	Airline Pilot $115,300

To the Teacher: Cut apart and have students draw a career card randomly. Allow no trades. This will be their career throughout the simulation. Alternate method: Allow students to choose their own careers and research the median salary of their chosen career.

Career Cards (cont.)

Computer Programmer $69,620	Insurance Agent $62,520	Bank Teller $23,610	Mail Carrier $50,250
Secretary $29,050	Police Sergeant $64,544	Flight Attendant $41,630	Dispensing Optician $34,800
Dental Assistant $654/week	Physician $186,040 (Primary Care)	Photographer $35,980	Waiter/ Waitress $400/week
Pharmacist $109,380	Public Relations Specialist $59,150	Cashier $380/week	Automotive Mechanic $675/week

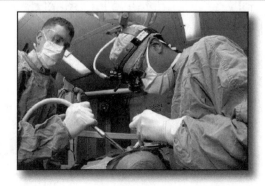

Name: _____ Date: _____

Welcome to the Working World!

Vocabulary to know:

Gross salary = all salary earned before taxes and deductions
Net salary = salary after taxes and deductions, "take home pay"
Tax = charge imposed by the government for public usage

Your new career is _____

Your yearly gross salary is _____

Compute the following and **show your work.**

1. What is your **weekly** gross salary? _____

2. Let's estimate that you pay 25% of your weekly gross salary in state and federal income taxes. This money is automatically deducted from your paycheck. How much do you pay in taxes every week?

   _____

3. What is your weekly **net** salary now? _____

4. Your employer also automatically takes the following deductions from your paycheck each month:

   Health insurance _____   Dental insurance _____

   Other (_____) _____

   Now, after all of these deductions, what is your monthly net salary? _____

5. Finally, after all of these important deductions that you can't control, what is your yearly net salary?

   _____

6. What is the difference in dollars between your yearly gross and net salaries? _____

IMPORTANT: SAVE THIS WORKSHEET FOR LATER USE IN THE SIMULATION.

Checks

A **checking account** lets you deposit your money in a bank, earn interest on it, and have constant access to it. Banks issue depositors checks, which work almost like cash. People write checks for the amount necessary to pay their debts. The person who receives the check signs the back **(endorses the check),** sends it to the bank, and the bank pays them that amount of money from the person's account. All banks talk to each other electronically through computers.

Checks can only be written and signed by the person whose name appears on the check. They should always be written in pen so the information cannot be changed. The following information must be written on every check: the date, the name of the person or business to be paid, the amount to be paid (in words and in numbers), and the signature of the person whose name appears on the check.

John Doe
#1 Easy Street
Anytown, MO 55555   Date _____

Pay to
the Order of _____ $ _____

_____ Dollars

The American Bank

Memo _____   _____

052000168   0203   000000   000

These numbers are the check routing numbers. These numbers tell the computers that read the check where the account is located in the United States.

The next six numbers (more or less depending upon your bank) are your account number.

Finally, the last group of numbers is your check number.

These numbers are the branch numbers. This tells the computer in exactly which branch of The American Bank your account is located.

Application for a Checking Account

CHECKING ACCOUNT APPLICATION

Customer 1			Customer 2 (only if joint account)		
Name (First) (Last)		Date of Birth	Name (First) (Last)		Date of Birth
Address		County	Address		County
City	State	Zip Code	City	State	Zip Code
Area Code/Home Phone	Area Code/Work Phone		Area Code/Home Phone	Area Code/Work Phone	
Driver's License No.	State	S.S. #	Driver's License No.	State	S.S. #
S.S.#/Year Issued	S.S.#/State Issued	Sex	S.S.#/Year Issued	S.S.#/State Issued	Sex
Employer	Occupation		Employer	Occupation	
Remarks			Remarks		

Account Information

Date	Account issued by	Branch No.
Amount of initial deposit	Account No.	

I hereby acknowledge that this account was opened according to my instructions. I understand the information presented to me, and I promise that the information furnished is true according to class information. I authorize the bank to check my credit and employment history, if necessary.

Customer 1 signature	Date
Customer 2 signature (only if joint account)	Date

To the teacher: Have students complete the checking account application above before receiving checkbook materials. Each student should initially deposit an amount equal to two months' net pay (as figured in the prior activity). The teacher should check over each application, issue an account number, and distribute checkbook materials once the application is accepted.

Blank Checks

Staple here   Staple here   Staple here   Staple here   Staple here

Date _____

Pay to
the Order of _____ $ _____

_____ Dollars

The American Bank

Memo _____   _____

052000168   0203

Staple here   Staple here   Staple here   Staple here   Staple here

Date _____

Pay to
the Order of _____ $ _____

_____ Dollars

The American Bank

Memo _____   _____

052000168   0203

Staple here   Staple here   Staple here   Staple here   Staple here

Date _____

Pay to
the Order of _____ $ _____

_____ Dollars

The American Bank

Memo _____   _____

052000168   0203

To the student: Cut out all of your checks. Write your name, account number, and check number on each of your checks. Place in order and staple with your deposit slips at the bottom half of your folded checkbook cover.

To the teacher: Copy at least five pages of checks for each student. Provide students with a checkbook cover 6" square. Ideally, this should be made out of a sturdy paper and laminated for durability.

Deposit Slips

Staple here   Staple here   Staple here   Staple here   Staple here

DEPOSIT TICKET

Cash	
Checks	
Total	
-Cash	
Net Deposit	

Date _____

DEPOSITS MAY NOT BE AVAILABLE FOR IMMEDIATE WITHDRAWAL

_____

SIGN HERE FOR CASH RECEIVED (IF REQUIRED)

The American Bank

052000168   0203

Staple here   Staple here   Staple here   Staple here   Staple here

DEPOSIT TICKET

Cash	
Checks	
Total	
-Cash	
Net Deposit	

Date _____

DEPOSITS MAY NOT BE AVAILABLE FOR IMMEDIATE WITHDRAWAL

_____

SIGN HERE FOR CASH RECEIVED (IF REQUIRED)

The American Bank

052000168   0203

Staple here   Staple here   Staple here   Staple here   Staple here

DEPOSIT TICKET

Cash	
Checks	
Total	
-Cash	
Net Deposit	

Date _____

DEPOSITS MAY NOT BE AVAILABLE FOR IMMEDIATE WITHDRAWAL

_____

SIGN HERE FOR CASH RECEIVED (IF REQUIRED)

The American Bank

052000168   0203

To the student: Cut out all of your deposit slips and staple behind your checks. Don't forget to fill in your account number. Complete one of these every time you have money to deposit into your account.

To the teacher: Copy at least two pages of deposit slips for each student. Provide a box for collecting deposit slips and a box for checks paid. These can be used to complete the bank statements later in the simulation.

Checkbook Register

To the Student: Cut out your checkbook registers. Fold them together on the dashed middle line and staple to the inside top of your checkbook cover.

Staple here	Staple here	Staple here		Staple here	Staple here	
CHECK NUMBER	DATE	DESCRIPTION OF TRANSACTION	✓	PAYMENT/ DEBT	DEPOSIT/ CREDIT	BALANCE
				$	$	$
				$	$	$
				$	$	$
				$	$	$
				$	$	$
				$	$	$
				$	$	$
				$	$	$
				$	$	$
				$	$	$
				$	$	$
				$	$	$
				$	$	$
				$	$	$
				$	$	$

To the Teacher: Make at least 2 copies of the checkbook register for each student.

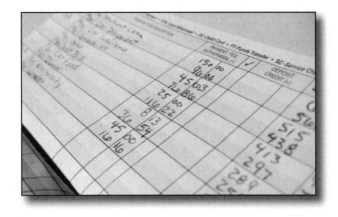

Money Cards

Your car breaks down. Pay Good Guy Towing Company $50.	You adopt a cat. Pay the adoption agency $55 for fees.	You buy a winning lottery ticket. Win $150.	You need a new tire for your car. Buy one for $156.95 from Tires 4 U.
Your grandmother sends you a check for $25.	You go to the amusement park for the day. Pay $46.99.	You fly home for Christmas on Frigid Flyers Airlines. Buy a ticket for $245.90.	You need a new pair of jeans. Pay Jesse Jeans and Company $32.76.
You stop at Gas on the Go for gas. It costs $38.75 to fill up your tank.	Your library books are overdue. Write a check to Lend-me City Library for $5.10.	You buy a new television from TV Tech for $199.98.	You need to pay your car insurance. Pay Super Duper Insurance Company $98.67.
You take a friend out to dinner and pay by check. You owe Pizza Plus $21.69.	You receive your income tax refund in the amount of $400.	You get a rebate check in the mail for $20.	Your boss gives you a $225 Christmas bonus.

To the Teacher: These cards can be used at any time during the simulation. Students should randomly draw a money card and then make the appropriate notation in their checkbooks. Cards can be returned to the pile or discarded. Don't forget to use a central collection box for all student checks and deposits. This system allows for checks to be "cancelled" and returned to the students when they receive their bank statements.

Money Cards (cont.)

You lose your dog and place an ad in the Anytown Blab to find him. The ad costs $18.75.	You need x-rays on your broken foot. Pay Med-X $146.00.	You win a raffle. Collect $500.	You buy your mother a birthday present at Priceless Perfumes. Write a check for $40.
You pay Trouble-free Travel $635 for a bus trip to the mountains.	You lose your watch and have to buy another one. Pay Tickin' Time $36.99.	Your brother Jimmy asks you to loan him $50, and you say yes. Write him a check.	Pay your electric bill. Write a check for $76.34 to Central Electric Company.
It's your birthday and you receive $62 as a present from your parents.	Your cat needs an operation to save his life. Pay Dr. Longlife $379.	You buy a new novel at Books and Books Bookstore. Pay $19.95.	You and your date go to the movies. You pay Big Screen Theaters $15.50.
You buy a picture to hang above your new couch. Pay Hangin' Around Wall Works $47.00.	You owe the newspaper for your subscription. Pay the Anytown Blab $27.	You receive a check for $45 from a neighbor for rescuing her prize-winning pet potbellied pig.	Your brother pays you back the $50 he borrowed.

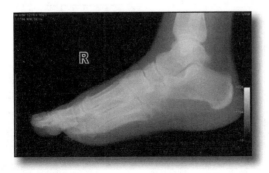

Name: _____   Date: _____

How to Balance Your Checkbook

Every month you should reconcile your bank statement with your checkbook. **Reconcile** means to make sure that both agree with each other. Follow the steps below to balance your checkbook each month.

1. Check off every withdrawal, check paid, and deposit on your bank statement in your checkbook.

2. Make sure that there is nothing left on the bank statement that you forgot to write in your checkbook.

3. Note and deduct any account fees for the month.

4. Write any deposits you made that do not appear on the bank statement here.

Date	Amount
_____	_____
_____	_____
_____	_____
_____	_____ Total = _____

5. Write any checks you wrote or withdrawals you made that do not appear on the bank statement here.

Date   Amount

_____   _____

_____   _____

_____   _____

_____   _____

_____   _____

_____   _____   Total = _____

6. Write your ending balance from the bank statement here.   _____

7. Add the total from #4.   + _____

                                                       = _____

8. Subtract the total from #5   - _____

9. This number should match the balance in your checkbook!   = _____

Bank Statement

The American Bank

Branch Number 0203	Account Number
Starting Date	Ending Date

Mail to:

Page 1 of 2

Withdrawals

Date	Check Number or Teller Withdrawal	Amount
_____	_____	_____
_____	_____	_____
_____	_____	_____
_____	_____	_____
_____	_____	_____
_____	_____	_____
_____	_____	_____
_____	_____	_____
_____	_____	_____
_____	_____	_____

To the Teacher: This page can be used in several ways. I suggest copying one for each student after several banking transactions have been made. Return the contents of the "bank" boxes to the students and have them swap returned checks and deposits to complete the necessary information on their partner's bank statement. Partners then trade back bank statements and each "balances" his or her checkbook using the prepared bank statement.

Bank Statement (cont.)

The American Bank

Branch Number 0203	Account Number
Starting Date	Ending Date

Page 2 of 2

Deposits

Date	Deposit Amount
_____	_____
_____	_____
_____	_____
_____	_____
_____	_____

Summary of Account

Beginning Balance	_____
+ Total Deposits	_____
- Total Checks and Withdrawals	_____
- Account Fees	_____
Ending Balance	_____

Credit Cards

Credit cards are a commonly used method of payment around the world. Banks issue credit cards to customers they trust. When a customer uses a **credit card**, the bank pays for the customer's purchases temporarily (like a short-term loan). It then sends the customer a statement each month accounting for all of the charges on the credit card that month. The customer can either pay the bank in full and be charged no interest on the loan, or he can pay only a portion and pay interest on the rest of the unpaid amount. Some sources estimate that over 80% of all transactions are made by checks or credit cards.

Banks reserve the right to deny credit to any customer that they feel is a bad risk (might be unable to pay). They also set credit limits on cards. These are the maximum amounts cardholders may owe at once. Banks like to issue credit cards since many consumers do not pay their bills in full every month and end up paying interest to the bank.

The American Bank

2001 6000 5281 ☐☐☐☐

Valid From   Good Thru

_____   _____

_____   **Chargit**

Customer Service: 1-800-555-9000

Authorized Signature

If found send to: The American Bank

The American Bank

3020 5200 1263 ☐☐☐☐

Valid From   Good Thru

_____   _____

_____   **SpendN**

Customer Service: 1-800-555-9000

Authorized Signature

If found send to: The American Bank

To the Teacher: Copy these credit cards and fill in different numbers to complete the last four digits of the account numbers. Have the students complete the information and sign on the back. Fold and laminate credit cards for the students upon credit application acceptance.

Credit Card Application

Yes! Please send me an **American Bank** credit card! Check one: __ Chargit __ SpendN

Personal Information

Name (Last, First, Middle)		Street Address		
City	State	Zip Code	Years at address	__ Rent __ Own __ Live w/Parents
Date of Birth	Mother's Maiden Name	Home Phone and Area Code		Are you a U.S. resident? __ Yes __ No
Previous Address	City	State	Zip Code	Years there

Employment Information

Employer		Position	
Work Address	City	State	Zip Code
Work Phone and Area Code	Social Security Number	Years at this employer	

Income Information

Your yearly income from all sources must be at least $8,000 to be considered for credit card acceptance.	Your total personal yearly income $
Other household yearly income $	Other yearly income sources $

Account Information

Checking Account Institution Name	Account Number
Savings Account Institution Name	Account Number

Check those that apply:

__ Wondercard __ Chargit __ SpendN __ Dept. Store __ Diner's Club __ Gasoline __ Other

Would you like an additional card at no charge? If yes, print full name to appear on card

By signing, I authorize The American Bank to check my credit history. I attest that the above information is true. I have read and understand the terms of credit.	Applicant's Signature X	Date

Credit Card Statement

The American Bank
Credit Card Division
Account Statement

Chargit

SpendN

Statement date _____

Cardholder's Name _____

Address _____

City, State, Zip _____

Account Number _____

Previous Balance $ _____

Interest = Amount x (18% ÷ 12 months) $ _____

New Purchases

_____ $ _____
_____ $ _____
_____ $ _____
_____ $ _____
_____ $ _____
_____ $ _____
_____ $ _____
_____ $ _____
_____ $ _____
_____ $ _____
_____ $ _____
_____ $ _____

Total of New Purchases $ _____
New Balance $ _____
Minimum Amount Due (10%) $ _____
Amount Paid $ _____
Remaining Balance $ _____

To the teacher: This activity can be done as a whole group with purchases filled in before copying or individually with pairs checking over each other's calculations.

Name: _____ Date: _____

Buying a Car

Your next step is to buy a car. Most people don't have enough money to buy a car outright (pay for it in full), so they take out a car loan. Then they can pay a little at a time each month for the car. Remember, they do have to pay extra interest to the bank for the loan. Most car loans are from 36 months (3 years) to 60 months (5 years) long.

The newspaper is one important place to look when thinking about buying a car. Usually, there is a special automotive section one or two days a week. For this activity, you will need the automotive section of the newspaper. You may also find information on cars for sale online.

Look through the automotive section and pick out a car you would like. Find the estimated purchase price of that car. Although most people negotiate on car prices, we will work with the actual ticket price. Follow the example and complete the chart to figure some estimated monthly payments assuming 4% interest. *Be sure to show your calculations on a separate sheet or on the back.*

Example
Purchase Price x % of Tax = Tax
Purchase Price + Tax = Loan Amount
Loan Amount x Interest Rate x Time of Loan = Interest
Loan Amount + Interest = Total Cost
Total Cost ÷ Number of Months of the Loan = Monthly Car Payment

---

	3 Years	4 Years	5 Years
Purchase Price			
Tax (7%)			
Loan Amount			
Interest Rate	4%	4%	4%
Interest			
Total Cost			
Number of Months			
Monthly Payment			

Name: _____ Date: _____

Buying a Car (cont.)

	3 Years	4 Years	5 Years
Purchase Price			
Tax (7%)			
Loan Amount			
Interest Rate	3%	5%	6%
Interest			
Total Cost			
Number of Months			
Monthly Payment			

To the teacher: Have the students complete this activity individually and then swap with a partner to check calculations.

Car Loan Application

Car Loan Application

Name _____

Address _____

City, State, Zip Code _____

Home Phone (____) _____

Employer _____

Work Address _____

City, State, Zip Code _____

Work Phone (____) _____

Total Monthly Income $ _____

Mortgage/Rent $ _____

Other Loan Payments $ _____

Credit Card _____ Account Number _____

Card Balance $ _____

Bank Name _____ City, State _____

Checking Balance $ _____ Savings Account # _____

Name of nearest living relative _____

Address _____

Phone (_____)_____ Relationship_____

Cost of Auto $ _____

Interest Cost $_____ Total Loan Amount $ _____

Number of Monthly Payments _____ Monthly Payments $ _____

I attest that the above information is true and complete. I promise to repay the lender in full and with interest.

Signature of Applicant X_____

Date _____

To the Teacher: Approve loans with monthly payments that, together with rent, equal less than 55% of total net monthly income.

Name: _____ Date: _____

Apartment Hunting

The next step to becoming independent is to find your own apartment. This can be both exciting and terrifying when you do it for the very first time. What do you need to know to locate and rent your first home? Read on . . .

The most common place to look for apartments for rent is in the classified section of the newspaper. There are also sites online where people can list properties for rent, similar to classified ads. The **classified section** is the "small print" of the newspaper where people advertise jobs, real estate, furniture, and all sorts of other things to be bought or sold. At first glance, the classified section may seem terribly confusing, but with a quick lesson on the "lingo," you'll be doing just fine!

Look in the classified section of a newspaper. Work with a partner to define the following abbreviations and terms.

1. duplex _____

2. bdrm. _____

3. util. _____

4. lg. _____

5. lux. _____

6. efficiency _____

7. a.c. _____

8. yd. _____

9. w/ _____

10. pd. _____

11. 3-2-2 _____

12. dep. _____

13. WBFP _____

14. W/D conn. _____

15. w/w carpet _____

16. mo. _____

17. apts. _____

18. TS kit. or EIK _____

19. mini blds. _____

20. fncd. _____

Apartment Application

About You   Date when filled out _____

Full Name _____

Current Address_____

_____

Phone (_____) _____

Apartment Name_____ Management Phone # (_____) _____

Current Monthly Rent $_____ Date Moved In_____

Social Security #_____

Driver's License # _____

Marital Status: ____ Single ____ Married ____ Divorced/Widowed ____ Separated

Birth date_____ Height ___Sex ___ Weight ___ Hair Color ____ Eye Color_____

Previous Address_____

_____

Apartment Name_____ Management Phone # (_____) _____

Previous Monthly Rent $_____ Date Moved In_____

Your Work

Present Employer_____

Work Address _____

_____

Work Phone (_____) _____ Type of Work _____

Monthly Income $_____ Date Started _____

Supervisor's Name _____

Previous Employer _____

Work Address _____

_____

Work Phone (_____) _____ Type of Work _____

Monthly Income $_____ Date Started_____

Supervisor's Name _____

Continued on next page.

Apartment Application (cont.)

Your Vehicles

Make of Vehicle _____ Year _____ License # _____ State _____

Make of Vehicle _____ Year _____ License # _____ State _____

Your Credit/Criminal History

Your Bank's Name _____ City, State _____

Checking Account # _____ Savings Account # _____

Have you ever: ____ been evicted or asked to move out?____ broken a rental contract or

lease contract?____ declared bankruptcy?____ been sued for nonpayment of rent?

_____ been convicted of a felony?

Other Information

Will you have a pet?_____If yes, what kind?_____

In the event of an emergency, please notify _____

Address and Phone_____

_____

Relationship _____

I declare that all statements above are true and complete. I authorize this apartment complex to verify them through whatever means necessary. Giving false information could be a criminal offense. The apartment complex is entitled to reject this application if I have given false information.

Applicant's signature _____

Signature of Apartment's Representative _____

Date Signed _____

Name: _____ Date: _____

Apartment Move-In Costs

There are a lot of things to think about when you move into a new apartment. There are loads of "hidden costs" that add into the picture. Use this planning guide as you get ready to "move" into your new apartment.

☐ Choose an apartment from the classified ads. You may choose to live with a roommate. Clip the classified ad from the newspaper.

☐ Each occupant of the apartment should complete an apartment application.

☐ Turn in the completed application(s), along with the classified ad of the apartment you choose, to your teacher. Remember that your lease will not be approved if your rent is more than 35% of your net monthly income. Aim to keep it around 25% of your income.

☐ Call the apartment that you have chosen to find out what the security deposit is on your apartment.

☐ Call the phone company to find out the charges to begin service.

☐ Call the electric company to find out the charges to begin service.

☐ Write checks to the apartment complex, the telephone company, and the electric company. If you have a roommate, divide the costs equally.

Expenses

Rent _____

Security deposit _____

Telephone _____

Electric _____

TOTAL MOVE-IN COSTS _____

Name: _____ Date: _____

What Do You Need?

For this activity, you will need a general department store catalog or you can search for prices online. Ask yourself what items you will need to move into an apartment on your own. What things can't you live without? Which do you already own? Which can you get for free from friends or relatives? Which will you have to buy? Try to be as realistic as possible. List the items under the proper category, and if necessary, figure out the cost of each item you will have to buy. Roommates should work together on this activity.

Kitchen

H G B _____ $ _____
H G B _____ $ _____
H G B _____ $ _____
H G B _____ $ _____
H G B _____ $ _____
H G B _____ $ _____
H G B _____ $ _____
H G B _____ $ _____
H G B _____ $ _____
H G B _____ $ _____

Key

H = Have item
G = Can get item from family/friends
B = Buy items

Bedroom

H G B _____ $ _____
H G B _____ $ _____
H G B _____ $ _____
H G B _____ $ _____
H G B _____ $ _____
H G B _____ $ _____
H G B _____ $ _____
H G B _____ $ _____
H G B _____ $ _____
H G B _____ $ _____

Name: _____ Date: _____

What Do You Need? (cont.)

Bathroom

H G B_____ $ _____

H G B_____ $ _____

H G B_____ $ _____

H G B_____ $ _____

H G B_____ $ _____

H G B_____ $ _____

H G B_____ $ _____

H G B_____ $ _____

H G B_____ $ _____

H G B_____ $ _____

Key

H = Have item
G = Can get item from
family/friends
B = Buy items

Living/Dining

H G B_____ $ _____

H G B_____ $ _____

H G B_____ $ _____

H G B_____ $ _____

H G B_____ $ _____

H G B_____ $ _____

H G B_____ $ _____

H G B_____ $ _____

H G B_____ $ _____

H G B_____ $ _____

TOTAL OF ALL NECESSARY PURCHASES

$ _____

Name: _____ Date: _____

Comparison Grocery Shopping

Now that you are all moved in, how about buying something to eat? Food is a necessity of life and can get quite expensive unless you know how to be a smart shopper. Comparison shop at two nearby grocery stores to discover which has the lower prices. List 15 food items. Be specific: include brand names and sizes. Then check the prices of these items at two different stores. You may be able to compare prices online.

Store #1 _____	Food Item	Store #2 _____
_____	_____	_____
_____	_____	_____
_____	_____	_____
_____	_____	_____
_____	_____	_____
_____	_____	_____
_____	_____	_____
_____	_____	_____
_____	_____	_____
_____	_____	_____
_____	_____	_____
_____	_____	_____
_____	_____	_____
_____	_____	_____
_____	_____	_____

Store #1 Total = $ _____   Store #2 Total = $ _____

Where will you shop for low prices? _____

Taxes and W-2 Forms

Form W-2 Wage and Tax Statement

Employer's name and address	Employee's name and address
Employer's identification number 59-8569554	Employee's social security number
wages, tips, and other compensation	Income tax withheld

Form W-2 Wage and Tax Statement

Employer's name and address	Employee's name and address
Employer's identification number 59-8569554	Employee's social security number
wages, tips, and other compensation	Income tax withheld

To the teacher: To complete the tax activity, you will need several copies of the 1040EZ tax pamphlet. The tax form in this book is a simplified version and may not match the current IRS tax form. Students will first need to complete their W-2 forms. Completing the actual tax forms works best as a whole-class activity. I also suggest the use of an overhead transparency to help students follow along.

Tax Form

Form **1040EZ**	## Income Tax Return for ## Single Filers With No Dependents

Name and Address

Name (first, initial, last)	Your social security number
Home address	☐☐☐ ☐☐ ☐☐☐
City, State, Zip Code	

Report your income

1. Total wages, salaries, and tips. See your W-2 form. ☐☐,☐☐☐.☐☐

2. Taxable interest income of $1,500 or less. ☐☐☐.☐☐

3. Add lines 1 and 2. This is your **adjusted gross income.** ☐☐,☐☐☐.☐☐

4. Can your parents (or someone else) claim you on their return?
   _____ Yes. See tax pamphlet for information.
   _____ No. Enter 9,350.00. This is the total of your
   standard deduction and personal exemption. ☐,☐☐☐.☐☐

5. Subtract line 4 from line 3. If line 4 is larger than line 3,
   enter 0. This is your **taxable income.** ☐☐,☐☐☐.☐☐

Figure your tax

6. Enter your Federal income tax withheld on your W-2 form(s). ☐☐,☐☐☐.☐☐

7. **Tax.** Look at line 5 above. Use the amount on **line 5** to find
   your tax in the tax table in the tax return pamphlet. Then
   enter the tax from the table on this line. ☐☐,☐☐☐.☐☐

Refund or amount you owe

8. If line 6 is larger than line 7, subtract line 7 from line 6.
   This is your **refund.** ☐,☐☐☐.☐☐

9. If line 7 is larger than line 6, subtract line 6 from line 7. This
   is the **amount you owe.** Attach your payment for full amount
   payable to the "Internal Revenue Service." Write your name,
   address, social security number, daytime phone number, and
   "Tax Form 1040EZ" on it. ☐,☐☐☐.☐☐

Sign your return

I have read this return. I declare that it is true, correct, and complete to the best of my knowledge.

Your signature   Date

X _____   _____

Answer Keys

What is Economics? (page 2)
Sample answers:
water: plentiful, renewable
oil: relatively plentiful, nonrenewable
diamonds: scare, nonrenewable

Goods and Services (page 3)
Sample answers:
Goods: automobiles, air conditioners, clothing, computers
Services: restaurants, doctors, cleaners, pet grooming

The Chicken Farm (page 5)
1. Approximately 4 dozen (50 eggs); high; scarcity; high
2. 12.5 dozen (150 eggs); low; surplus; low

The New and Improved Chicken Farm (page 7)
1. The number of chicken farms will increase because more farmers will see selling eggs as a good way to make money due to the high price of eggs.
2. The supply of eggs will increase.
3. This will lower the demand for eggs and therefore lower the cost of eggs.
4. Once the price of eggs is driven back down by the surplus, the number of chicken farms will fall again because they cannot afford to stay in business at the lower price.
5. This is a circular cycle because as price goes up, supply goes up. Once supply goes up, however, demand decreases, which in turn lowers the price once again. Lower prices usually mean lowered supplies, which can eventually drive demand and prices up yet again.

Case Study: Auctions (page 8)
1. There are so many bidders because the price is low.
2. Law of Demand (as price decreases, demand increases)
3. So many bidders have dropped out because the price has gone up. As price increases, the demand for an item usually decreases.
4. Many bidders drove the final price of the vase up.
5. The Law of Supply states that as price increases, supply increases. As a result of the high price the vase brought this week, more people should bring vases to sell next week.
6. An increase in the supply of vases will lower their demand. Lowered demand usually forces sellers to lower prices. This happens because they are in surplus (there are more vases than people who want to buy them).

Case Study: Write Your Own (page 9)
Answers will vary

More Economic Terms (page 10)
2, 4, 3, 5, 8, 6, 1, 7

Case Study: The Lemonade Stand (pages 11–12)
1. selling a good
2. Sample answers: water, lemons, sugar
3. plentiful
4. renewable
5. Sample answer: Materials are bought at store. Lemons are cut and squeezed into pitcher. Water is added. Sugar is added as necessary. Lemonade is chilled.
6. Sample answers: lemon growers, sugarcane growers, sugar producers, water companies, and so on

7. Demand is three people
8. Sample answers: hot weather, busy location, lack of other drink stands nearby, etc.
9. Sample answers: cool weather or rain, too many other drink stands nearby, slow location, etc.
10. If the price of lemonade increases due to greater demand, other people might decide to sell lemonade, too. (Increased supply could lower overall demand, driving prices back down again.)
11. If the price of lemonade decreases due to a lesser demand, more people might want to buy lemonade. (However, fewer sellers will be able to afford to sell it at the reduced price. This may cause a decrease in supply, raising prices once again.)
12. Competition usually increases supply, decreases demand, and lowers prices.

Money Research Project (page 14)

$1	George Washington/The Great Seal
$2	Thomas Jefferson/Signing of the Declaration of Independence
$5	Abraham Lincoln/Lincoln Memorial
$10	Alexander Hamilton/U.S. Treasury
$20	Andrew Jackson/The White House
$50	Ulysses S. Grant/U.S. Capitol
$100	Benjamin Franklin/Independence Hall

How to Calculate Interest (page 16)

1. $1,900
2. $23.75
3. approximately $255.16
4. $2,150

The Federal Reserve (page 18)

1. The Federal Reserve was established to strengthen the nation's banking activities by protecting bank deposits and controlling the money supply.
2. Federal Reserve banks get their money by requiring all smaller banks to deposit a portion of their money with them.
3. Banks loan out all money not held in reserve in order to make money from the interest charged.
4. All depositors cannot withdraw their accounts at once because the bank has loaned part of that money out and does not have sufficient funds on hand to cover all their accounts.
5. The Federal Reserve affects the money supply by setting and changing the amount of money banks are required to hold in reserve, by buying and selling bonds, and by making emergency loans to banks low on funds.
6. Answers may vary. Sample answer: The Federal Reserve wants to control recession/inflation. It also wants to establish faith in the national economy.
7. Inflation (rising demand, rising prices) is the result of too much money in circulation.
8. Recession (decreasing demand, falling prices) is the result of too little money in circulation.

Federal Reserve Banks (page 19)

1.	Dallas	2.	Chicago
3.	Saint Louis	4.	Boston
5.	Cleveland	6.	Atlanta
7.	New York	8.	Minneapolis
9.	Kansas City	10.	San Francisco
11.	Richmond	12.	Philadelphia

Map should be labeled accordingly.

Flow Chart: The Federal Reserve (page 20)

increased reserves	decreased reserves
raise	lower
decreases	increases
decreases	increases
decreases	increases
decreases	increases
decreases	increases

Inflation (page 22)

1. The Federal Reserve most affects the money supply.
2. There is a decrease in production during a recession due to the decrease in money in circulation, decreased demand, and falling prices.
3. There is an increase in production during inflation due to the increase in money in circulation, increased demand, and rising prices.
4. The dollar is worth comparatively less during inflation because prices are going up, meaning that the same dollar buys less than before.
5. The dollar is worth comparatively more during a recession because demand has decreased, causing prices to fall. Falling prices mean that the dollar can buy more than it did before.
6. The process is circular because when a recession causes too much unemployment and lowered demand, the Federal Reserve increases the money supply to stop the recession. This triggers inflation, which means prices rise. When prices rise too much or too quickly, the Federal Reserve will halt the inflation by lowering the money supply, triggering another recession.

Inflation Case Study: Real Estate (page 23)

Recession: Supply 3, Demand 2
1. Too little
2. Down
3. Decreased demand drives prices down.
4. Up

Inflation: Supply 3, Demand 4
5. Too much
6. Up
7. Increased demand drives prices up.
8. Down

What Did Things Cost (page 24)

Answers will vary.

Case Study: Menus (page 25)

1. grilled cheese sandwich, roast beef sandwich, fresh fruit, lemonade
2. lemonade
3. ham and cheese sandwich, turkey club, potato chips, french fries, giant cookie, soda, milk
4. potato chips, turkey club, French fries
5. approximately 12.59%
6. deflation

Economic Crossword Puzzle (pages 26–27)

ACROSS:
2. recession
5. denomination
7. scarce
8. loan
9. surplus
10. supply
12. inflation
16. economics
17. bank
18. nonrenewable
20. good
21. consumer
22. service
23. Federal Reserve

DOWN:
1. producer
3. interdependence
4. depression
6. consumption
11. interest
13. mint
14. demand
15. renewable
19. resource

Matching Quiz: Economic Terms (page 28)

1.	E	13.	D
2.	L	14.	N
3.	F	15.	M
4.	H	16.	O
5.	C	17.	T
6.	J	18.	W
7.	B	19.	R
8.	U	20.	P
9.	S	21.	A
10.	V	22.	K
11.	I	23.	Q
12.	G		

Welcome to the Working World (page 32)
Answers will vary.

How to Balance Your Checkbook (page 40)
Answers will vary.

Apartment Hunting (page 49)
1. house for two families
2. bedroom
3. utilities
4. large
5. luxury
6. one-room apartment (living/dining/sleep-ing area all in one)
7. air conditioning
8. yard
9. with
10. paid
11. 3 bedrooms, 2 bathrooms, 2-car garage
12. deposit
13. wood-burning fireplace
14. washer/dryer connection
15. wall-to-wall carpet
16. month
17. apartments
18. table-space kitchen; eat-in kitchen
19. mini blinds
20. fenced

Bibliography

Adler, David A. *Prices Go Up, Prices Go Down.* New York: Franklin Watts, 1984.

Andrews, Carolyn. *What Are Goods and Services?* (Economics in Action). New York: Crabtree Publishing Company, 2008.

Bach, G.L. and V. Clain-Stefanelli. "Money." *World Book Encyclopedia.* 1978, vol. 13, pp. 588–589.

Bochner, Arthur and Rose Bochner. *The New Totally Awesome Money Book for Kids,* Revised and Updated Edition. New York: Newmarket Press, 2007.

Derks, Scott, ed. *The Value of a Dollar: Prices and Incomes in the United States, 1860–2009.* 4th ed. Amenia, NY: Grey House Pub., 2009.

Godfrey, Neale S. *Ultimate Kid's Money Book.* New York: Aladdin, 2002.

Harman, Hollis Page. *Money Sense for Kids,* 2nd ed. Hauppauge, NY: Barron's Educational Series, 2005.

Heilbroner, Robert and Lester Thurow. *Economics Explained.* New York: Touchstone Books, 1998.

Lee, Susan. *ABZ's of Economics.* New York: Pocket, 1988.

Maybury, Richard J. *Whatever Happened to Penny Candy?* 6th ed. Placerville, California: Bluestocking Press, 2010.

Nelson, Murry R. *Children and Social Studies: Creative Teaching in the Elementary Classroom.* New York: Harcourt College Pub., 1992.

Schwartz, David M. *If You Made a Million.* New York: HarperCollins, 1994.

2010 1040EZ Forms and Instructions, The Department of the Treasury/Internal Revenue Service (Washington, D.C.: U.S. Government Printing Office, 2010).
found online at: http://www.irs.gov/pub/irs-pdf/f1040ez.pdf

Forms included in this book were adapted from those of Bank of America Texas N.A., Maryland National Bank, the Internal Revenue Service, and the Texas Apartment Association, Inc.